This book belongs to
Boodles' Buddy:

_____

_____

_____

For my firstborn and "bestest biggie" Andrew;
you are a great big brother!

For my sweet Matthew; I am so happy that Boodles
gets to share the pages of this book with you!

My Sunshines – this one is for the two of you!

I love you "to infinity," with "all of my heart."

Love, Mom

Published by

Purposeful Goods, LLC
99 Almaden Boulevard, Suite 500
San Jose, California 95113
purposefulgoods.com

We are having a baby!

Created by Christine Burger

Purposeful Goods™

Hi! My name is Boodles! You are growing up and getting bigger every day. Becoming a "big kid" is super-duper fun. You will have lots of questions and there will be many things you will want to know about. I'm here to be your Buddy and help explain them to you!

This is a very happy time because your mommy has a tiny seed growing in her tummy. A tiny baby is coming and that means that you are going to have a little brother or sister very soon. How exciting!

Yep, you are a "big kid" now. I call it being a "Biggie." Being a Biggie is such a fun and important job. As your Buddy, I want to help you be the best Biggie you can be.

One of the best things about being a Biggie is that you get to be a super-duper helper for Mommy and Daddy. Being your Buddy means that I get to be a super-duper helper, too!

Sometimes Mommy will get tired as Baby grows in her tummy.

Let's help Mommy by playing together quietly so she can rest.

We can play make-believe and have lots of adventures!

We can build a fort with blankets and have a tea party with all your stuffed animal friends. We will have so much fun!

Mommy will go visit a baby doctor. The doctor will listen to Baby's heart and measure how big Baby is getting. Maybe we can go with Mommy to visit the doctor and listen to Baby's heart, too!

As Baby grows, Mommy's tummy will get bigger and bigger. This will make it hard for Mommy to pick you up. But we can still hug and kiss Mommy. We can even talk to Baby. Baby can hear you from inside Mommy's tummy. Baby will remember your voice and already know and love you when she or he is born!

There are so many fun ways we can prepare for Baby's arrival!

Baby will need a lot of things, like clothes, blankets, diapers, bottles, and maybe a swing. We can help Mommy and Daddy pick out all the supplies at the store.

We can help them wash Baby's clothes and put everything where it belongs.

Baby will need something super-duper special to wear home from the hospital.

We can help Mommy pick out the perfect outfit!

Baby will also need a car seat to ride in. We can watch Daddy install it in the back seat. You and Baby will get to ride next to each other!

When Baby comes home, he or she will sleep a whole bunch. At first, Baby may sleep in a little bed next to Mommy and Daddy's bed, called a bassinet.

After that, maybe you will get to share your room with Baby!

Since you are a Biggie now and I am your Buddy, we can help Mommy and Daddy find the most peaceful place for Baby. Maybe we can help decorate it with soft toys and cuddly animals.

Your little brother or sister will need a name! Picking a name is super-duper important. Most names have a meaning. Ask Mommy and Daddy what your name means. We can help Mommy and Daddy think of lots of names, so they can make a list of boy names and girl names. When Baby is born, Mommy and Daddy will know just the right name to choose.

At first, Baby will be fragile. Do you know what fragile means? That means Baby could get hurt very easily, so we must be very gentle. It is super-duper important that we don't touch the top of Baby's head, which is soft and still growing. Maybe Mommy can show you on my head where the soft spot is on Baby's head.

Baby will not be very strong at first. Mommy and Daddy will show you how to hold Baby. Maybe we can practice together. Ask Mommy to put me in your arms. I know you are going to do a great job!

When Baby is ready to arrive, Mommy will go to the hospital.

Mommy and Daddy will have a plan for you and me. Maybe we will stay with

Grandma and Grandpa while Daddy takes Mommy to the hospital.

We will have so much fun waiting for Baby to be born!

Mommy may have to stay in the hospital for a couple of days. Since you are a Biggie and I'm your Buddy, we can be Daddy's super-duper helpers! We can help him by doing things around the house and by being on our best behavior.

Finally, when it is time, we will go to the hospital to meet your new brother or sister.

You will get to hold Baby for the first time.

I just know you will be the very best Biggie ever!

And I will be your very best Buddy ever!

Because "everybody needs a buddy sometimes," Christine Burger created *Your Buddy Boodles*. Boodles' motto, "I will wipe away your tears, chase away your fears and be there with good cheer." Teachable moments, tender explanations and embracing "the why," makes Boodles a parent's buddy too.

Founder of celebrated children's skin care brand Noodle & Boo, Christine has embraced her roles as a mom and an entrepreneur by continuing to find ways to use her personal experiences to create products for parents who also want the very best for their children. She truly believes, "There is nothing more wonderful or more important than caring for and loving a child."
Boodles would agree.